CR

Blake Shelton

ABDO
Publishing Company

Big Buddy BOOKS
Buddy Bios

by **Sarah Tieck**

VISIT US AT
www.abdopublishing.com

Published by ABDO Publishing Company, PO Box 398166, Minneapolis, Minnesota 55439.

Printed in the United States of America, North Mankato, Minnesota.
102012
012013

♲ PRINTED ON RECYCLED PAPER

Coordinating Series Editor: Rochelle Baltzer
Contributing Editors: Megan M. Gunderson, Marcia Zappa
Graphic Design: Maria Hosley
Cover Photograph: *AP Photo*: Tammie Arroyo.
Interior Photographs/Illustrations: *AP Photo*: Evan Agostini (pp. 17, 27), The Oklahoman, Jaconna Aguirre (p. 12),
    Isaac Brekken (p. 23), Julie Jacobson (p. 25), Peter Kramer (p. 17), Mike McCarn (p. 4), Wade Payne (p. 15), Matt
    Sayles, file (p. 21), Warner Bros. Records (p. 23); *Getty Images*: R. Diamond/WireImage (p. 11), Rick Diamond
    (p. 19), Christopher Polk/Getty Images for NBCUniversal (p. 29), Rusty Russell (p. 7); *Shutterstock*: Bryan
    Busovicki (p. 8), Creative Jen Designs (p. 19).

Cataloging-in-Publication Data

Tieck, Sarah.
  Blake Shelton: country music star / Sarah Tieck.
    p. cm. -- (Big buddy biographies)
  ISBN 978-1-61783-754-8
  1. Shelton, Blake, 1976- --Juvenile literature. 2. Country musicians--United States--Biography--Juvenile literature.   I.
Title.
  782.421642092--dc22
  [B]
                        2012946491

Contents

Blake is known for his live shows. He has performed at events such as NASCAR races.

Rising Star

Blake Shelton is a country singer. He has won awards for his hit albums and songs. Blake is also known for his work on the television show *The Voice*.

Where in the World?

Nebraska

Kansas

Missouri

New
Mexico

Oklahoma

• Ada

Arkansas

Texas

Louisiana

N
W   E
S

Family Ties

   Blake Tollison Shelton was born in Ada,
Oklahoma, on June 18, 1976. Blake's parents are
Dorothy and Dick Shelton. His older sister is Endy.
His older brother, Richie, died when Blake was a
teenager.

Blake and his wife, Miranda Lambert, wrote a song about Richie. It is called "Over You." It was released in 2012.

As Blake started out as a country singer, his family supported his dreams.

7

Nashville is known for country music. Many country stars start out there.

Did you know...

Blake's parents divorced. But, the family stayed close. They continued to spend time together on holidays.

Growing Up

When Blake was young, his mother owned a beauty salon. His father sold cars. Blake liked to sing and play the guitar.

In high school, Blake knew he wanted a career in music. So, he practiced his music and improved.

In 1994, Blake graduated from high school. Two weeks later, he moved to Nashville, Tennessee. There, he met people in the music business. They helped him record a demo and become a better performer.

First Album

In 2001, Blake **released** his first single. It was called "Austin." It became a major hit! Later that year, Blake released his first album.

Blake was excited for this moment. He'd been working very hard on his music. People took notice! In 2002, he was **nominated** for an Academy of Country Music (ACM) Award. Also, his album sold more than 500,000 copies. So, it was called a gold album.

Did you know...

Blake's first album is self-titled. This means it is called *Blake Shelton*.

Growing Talent

Blake kept working hard making music. In 2003, he **released** *The Dreamer*. This album had a hit song called "The Baby." And, it became a gold album!

Blake's third album came out in 2004 and also became a gold album. It is called *Blake Shelton's Barn and Grill*. In 2007, Blake released a fourth album. And the next year, his recording of "Home" became a hit song.

Later in 2008, Blake **released** *Startin' Fires*. This was his fifth major album. In 2009, he and singer Trace Adkins released "Hillbilly Bone." It was a hit song from Blake's sixth album, *Hillbilly Bone*. This album was released in 2010.

Blake and Trace often performed their hit song together.

Singing Star

Blake and Trace won awards for "Hillbilly Bone." They were honored by the ACM. And, they were **nominated** for a **Grammy Award**.

In 2010, Blake won two Country Music Association (CMA) Awards. He was especially excited to win the Male **Vocalist** of the Year award. This is an important honor.

Blake beat Brad Paisley to win the CMA Male Vocalist of the Year award. Brad had won it three years in a row!

Trace and Blake won a CMT Music Award for "Hillbilly Bone."

17

Country Legend

In 2010, Blake was asked to become a member of the Grand Ole Opry. This is an important honor. Only certain country singers are asked to join!

The Grand Ole Opry is famous for its country music **performances**. They can be viewed live on stage or on television. Also, they can be heard on the radio. The Grand Ole Opry radio show began in 1925.

Trace welcomed Blake to the Grand Ole Opry.

Some of the most famous country singers have been part of the Grand Ole Opry. They include Garth Brooks, Reba McEntire, and Carrie Underwood.

The Voice

In 2011, Blake got a new opportunity. He was asked to be a judge and voice **coach** on *The Voice*. This popular television show finds talented singers.

Each season begins with tryouts. Blake and three other judges choose small groups of finalists to coach. Then, the singers **perform** and **compete** against each other. The winner gets a record deal and $100,000.

Blake appears on *The Voice* with other well-known singers. They have included Christina Aguilera, Cee Lo Green, and Adam Levine.

BLAKE
SHELTON
RED RIVER BLUE

Big Hit

In 2011, Blake **released** a new song called "Honey Bee." Right away, it became a hit online. It continued to become more popular. Blake had never had a song become a hit so quickly!

Blake's album *Red River Blue* came out later that year. Fans were very excited to hear the rest of the album!

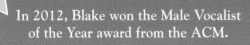

In 2012, Blake won the Male Vocalist of the Year award from the ACM.

Working Life

Blake spends many hours writing, recording, and practicing songs. He travels and performs live concerts.

Blake also works to be a good coach and judge on *The Voice*. He may spend many days on location for tapings. And, he works behind the scenes coaching singers for the show.

In 2011, Blake hosted the ACM Awards with Reba McEntire.

Off the Stage

In 2011, Blake married fellow country star Miranda Lambert. They spend free time at their farms in Oklahoma. They care for their animals. And, they see their friends and family. They also enjoy hunting and having parties.

Blake likes to work with groups that help people and animals. Sometimes, he and Miranda **perform** together at events to raise money or awareness.

In 2011, Blake and Miranda attended the CMA Awards. They both won awards that night!

Buzz

Blake's opportunities continue to grow. He and Miranda sang together at the 2012 Super Bowl. Blake also appeared on the third season of *The Voice* in fall 2012. Fans are excited to see what he'll do next!

Reporters often take Blake's picture.

Snapshot

★**Name**: Blake Tollison Shelton

★**Birthday**: June 18, 1976

★**Birthplace**: Ada, Oklahoma

★**Albums**: *Blake Shelton, The Dreamer, Blake Shelton's Barn and Grill, Startin' Fires, Hillbilly Bone, Red River Blue*

★**Appearances**: *Clash of the Choirs, The Voice*

Important Words

career work a person does to earn money for living.

coach someone who teaches or trains a person or a group on a certain subject or skill.

compete to take part in a contest between two or more persons or groups.

demo a recording to show a musical group or artist's abilities.

graduate (GRA-juh-wayt) to complete a level of schooling.

Grammy Award any of the awards given each year by the National Academy of Recording Arts and Sciences. Grammy Awards honor the year's best accomplishments in music.

guitar (guh-TAHR) a stringed musical instrument played by strumming.

nominate to name as a possible winner.

perform to do something in front of an audience. A performance is the act of doing something, such as singing or acting, in front of an audience.

release to make available to the public.

vocalist singer.

Web Sites

To learn more about Blake Shelton, visit ABDO Publishing Company online. Web sites about Blake Shelton are featured on our Book Links page. These links are routinely monitored and updated to provide the most current information available.

www.abdopublishing.com

Index